MW01065514

# The Multi-Colored Promise

*Brenna Phillips* (signature)

**Words by** Brenna Phillips

Illustrations **by Kristie Chamlee**

MISSIONAL PRESS
KIDS!

Smyrna, DE

Visit Missional Press's website at www.missional-press.com

Missional Press
149 Golden Plover Drive
Smyrna, DE  19977

ISBN 13 978-0-9825719-5-8
ISBN 10 0-9825719-5-X

Printed in the United States of America.

# Acknowledgements

A big thank you goes out to David for his Bible study preparation. Thank you for allowing me the creativity to turn those studies into children's books.

Thank you to Kristie Chamlee for turning the words of the popular Genesis story into colorful paintings. Your artistic talents are amazing for putting images with words. Our grandfathers would be proud of our partnership.

There once was a man named Noah. Noah wasn't the only man on earth. He lived with his wife and three sons and their wives.

*Genesis 5:32*

There were many men and women, but they were not making good choices. They were not following God's ways.

God was sorry he had made human beings on the earth.

*Genesis 6*

Noah was a good man, though, and he walked with God. He followed God's directions and guidance and made good choices.

*Genesis 6:9*

God told Noah he was going to destroy all the people on the earth, so he told Noah to build a boat for himself and his wife and his sons and their wives and many animals.

*Genesis 6:14*

God told Noah exactly how He wanted him to build the boat.

He told Noah to make it out of cypress wood 450 feet long, 75 feet wide, and 45 feet high; an opening at the top of the boat 18 inches from the edge of the roof down; a door on the side; upper, middle, and lower decks.

*Genesis 6:15-16*

Noah followed God's instructions to build the boat.

This boat did not need a rudder for steering. Noah was going to trust God to guide the boat in the right direction.

Then God told Noah to gather his family, including his wife and his three sons and their wives, on the boat because He was going to make the earth flood to destroy all living things.

*Genesis 6:17-20*

Noah did as God commanded him and gathered his family and every bird, animal, and crawling thing on the boat, along with food for his family and the animals.

*Genesis 6:20-21*

After Noah's family and the animals were all on the boat, the flood started.

Water rose from underground springs. The clouds in the sky poured out rain. The rain fell for 40 days and 40 nights covering the earth.

God destroyed every living thing on the land.

*Genesis 7:11-12*

The boat floated on water for many months. When the water receded and began to dry up and go away, the boat was able to finally land on the top of a mountain.

*Genesis 8:3-4*

Noah opened a window in the boat and sent out a raven. The bird flew until the water dried up.

*Genesis 8:6-7*

Then Noah sent out a dove but that bird came back because it could not find a place to land because of all the water.

*Genesis 8:8-9*

After 7 days, Noah sent the dove out again. It came back with an olive leaf in its mouth. Noah knew then that the ground was almost dry.

*Genesis 8:10-11*

After another 7 days, he sent the dove out again, but this time the bird did not come back.

*Genesis 8:12*

A few months later the land was completely dry and Noah removed the covering of the boat. He and his family and the animals got out of the boat.

*Genesis 8:13-19*

Noah built an altar of offerings to God. He gave thanks to God for saving him and his family and the animals from the flood.

*Genesis 8:20*

God was pleased with Noah and promised to never again destroy every living thing on the earth.

*Genesis 8:21*

*And God said, "This is the sign of the agreement between me and you and every living creature that is with you." Genesis 9:12*

LaVergne, TN USA
28 November 2010
205956LV00001B